Weather

by Ellen Lawrence

Consultant:

Judy Wearing, PhD, BEd
Faculty of Education, Queen's University
Ontario, Canada

BEARPORT
PUBLISHING

New York, New York

Credits

Cover, © Lipsky/Shutterstock and © Dmitry Zimin/Shutterstock; 3, © CoraMax/Shutterstock and © BillionPhotos.com/Shutterstock; 4L, © Blue Orange Studio/Shutterstock; 4C, © Chepko Danil Vitalevich/Shutterstock; 4–5, © Shutova Elena/Shutterstock and © Capricorn Studio/Shutterstock; 5, © CoraMax/Shutterstock and © MakC/Shutterstock; 6–7, © CoraMax/Shutterstock; 6, © Mega Pixel/Shutterstock; 7, © Vibrant Image Studio/Shutterstock and © Everything/Shutterstock; 8–9, © CoraMax/Shutterstock; 8, © dotini/Shutterstock; 9, © Mirexon/Shutterstock, © Svetlana Lukienko/Shutterstock, and © Kitch Bain/Shutterstock; 10–11, © CoraMax/Shutterstock and Ruby Tuesday Books; 11T, © Kletr/Shutterstock; 12–13, © CoraMax/Shutterstock and © Kutlayev Dmitry/Shutterstock; 13, © design56/Shutterstock; 14–15, © CoraMax/Shutterstock, © Lukas Gojda/Shutterstock, © Givaga/Shutterstock, © Imageman/Shutterstock, and © Peredniankina/Shutterstock; 14TL, © ARENA Creative/Shutterstock; 15, © endeavor/Shutterstock; 16–17, © CoraMax/Shutterstock, © STILLFX/Shutterstock, © CRSPIX/Shutterstock, and © Shebeko/Shutterstock; 17, © elsar/Shutterstock and © Somjork/Shutterstock; 18–19, © CoraMax/Shutterstock; 18, © Minerva Studio/Shutterstock and © dcwcreations/Shutterstock; 19, © ThamKC/Shutterstock and © r.classen/Shutterstock; 20–21, © kirbyedy/Shutterstock; 21, © ThamKC/Shutterstock and © r.classen/Shutterstock; 22TR, © Anita Patterson Peppers/Shutterstock; 22BL, © Tonis Valing/Shutterstock; 22BR, © Francesco Carucci/Shutterstock; 23, © Creative Travel Projects/Shutterstock, © Jamie Farrant/Shutterstock, © Smit/Shutterstock, © Andrey Popov/Shutterstock, and © Konstantin Shevtsov/Shutterstock.

Publisher: Kenn Goin
Editor: Jessica Rudolph
Creative Director: Spencer Brinker
Design: Emma Randall
Photo Researcher: Ruby Tuesday Books Ltd.

Library of Congress Cataloging-in-Publication Data in process at time of publication (2016)
Library of Congress Control Number: 2015040332
ISBN-13: 978-1-943553-18-1

For more information, write to Bearport Publishing Company, Inc., 45 West 21st Street, Suite 3B, New York, NY 10010.
Printed in the United States of America.

10 9 8 7 6 5 4 3 2 1

Contents

Let's Investigate Weather

What's the **weather** today? Is it sunny, rainy, or snowy? What's the **temperature**? Is it hot or cold? Paying attention to the weather helps us decide how to prepare for the day. On a hot, sunny day, you might put on shorts and a T-shirt and go to a beach. On a snowy day, you might wear a coat and hat and build a snowman. Inside this book are lots of fun experiments and cool facts about weather. So grab a notebook, and let's start investigating!

Check It Out!

Scientists called **meteorologists** watch and study the weather.
They also **forecast** what the weather will be like in the near future.
For one week, watch the weather like a meteorologist!

1. In a notebook, draw a weather chart like the one shown. Then put a **thermometer** outside.

2. Check the thermometer at the same time each day for a week. Write the temperatures in your chart.

3. At the end of each day, draw weather symbols to illustrate the weather for that day.

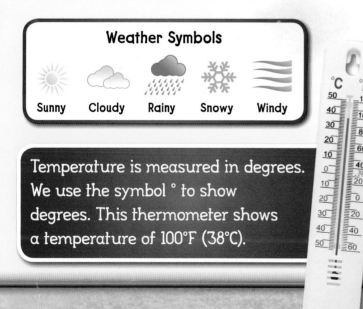

Weather Symbols

Sunny   Cloudy   Rainy   Snowy   Windy

Temperature is measured in degrees. We use the symbol ° to show degrees. This thermometer shows a temperature of 100°F (38°C).

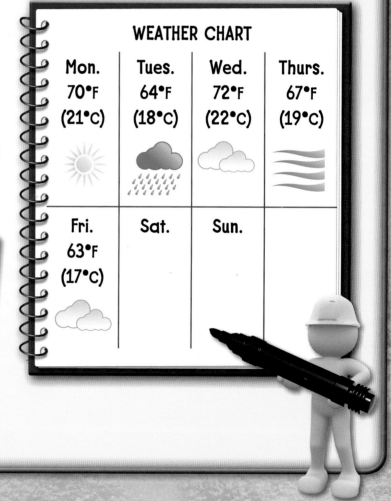

WEATHER CHART

Mon. 70°F (21°C)	Tues. 64°F (18°C)	Wed. 72°F (22°C)	Thurs. 67°F (19°C)
Fri. 63°F (17°C)	Sat.	Sun.	

How can the sun help you tell time?

Did you know the sun can help you tell time? Before clocks were invented, people used devices called sundials to figure out what time it was. You can make your own sundial and use it on a sunny day. Let's investigate!

You will need:

- A paper plate
- A marker or pen
- A pencil
- A watch or small clock
- A notebook and a pencil

 Fold a paper plate in half, press down on it, and unfold it. Then turn the plate halfway and fold it again to make a crease in the opposite direction. The creases should form a + shape.

2 Write the number 12 at the top of the plate on one of the creases.

12

3 Push a pencil through the center of the plate, so it's standing straight up.

 4 Just before noon on a sunny day, take your sundial and a clock or watch outdoors. Place the sundial in a sunny spot that's flat, with the number 12 facing up. The pencil will cast a shadow on the plate.

At exactly 12:00 P.M., position the sundial so the pencil's shadow is pointing to the number 12.

 5 At 1:00 P.M., note where the pencil's shadow is pointing and write a 1 at that spot on the top of the plate. Then at 2:00 P.M., check the shadow and write a 2, and so on.

6 Keep the sundial in the same place. Over the next day or so, in the morning or afternoon, check the sundial every hour and add the remaining numbers of a clock until you have all the numbers, 1 through 12. Now when it's sunny, you can use the sundial to tell time!

▶ Why do you think the pencil's shadow is moving?

▶ When wouldn't you be able to use a sundial to tell time?

Write down your ideas in your notebook.

(To learn more about this investigation and find the answers to the questions, see pages 20–21.)

How can you measure rainfall?

If you watch a weather report on TV, you might hear a meteorologist say how many inches of rain fell in a day. When it rains, the water trickles over roads and soaks into the soil. So how do scientists know how many inches of rain has fallen? They use a measuring device called a rain **gauge**. If you live in an area that gets regular rainfall, you can measure the amount of rain, too. Let's get measuring!

You will need:

- A clear glass or plastic container that has straight sides and is exactly the same width at the top and bottom
- A ruler
- A notebook and a pencil

rain gauge

Check the weather report each day. On a day when rain is **predicted**, place your container outside in an open area where it will collect rain.

▶ How many inches of rain were forecasted for the day?

Write the prediction in your notebook.

 Once the rain stops, check the container. Place a ruler against the outside of the container and measure the level of the water.

Record the measurement in your notebook.

▶ How many inches of rain fell?

▶ Did the measurement match the meteorologist's prediction?

(To learn more about this investigation and find the answers to the questions, see pages 20–21.)

How does water get into the clouds?

When the sky fills with **clouds**, we know it may soon rain. Yet where does the rainwater in clouds come from? It's all part of Earth's **water cycle**. In this next investigation, you will discover how the water cycle works. So grab your notebook and let's make some rain!

You will need:

- A large, clear glass or plastic bowl
- Water
- A ruler
- 4 small, heavy pebbles
- A clean, empty yogurt carton
- Plastic wrap
- A notebook and a pencil

 Pour 2 inches (5 cm) of water into the large bowl.

 Put three pebbles into the yogurt carton and stand the carton in the water in the center of the bowl. The pebbles should weigh down the carton so it doesn't float. Make sure there is no water in the yogurt carton.

Cover the top of the large bowl with plastic wrap so it's completely air tight.

 Place the fourth pebble in the center of the plastic wrap so the plastic dips down toward the yogurt carton.

5 Carefully place the bowl in a sunny spot, such as on a windowsill. After three days, check the bowl.

In your notebook, write down everything you observed.

▶ What do you see on the inside of the plastic wrap?

▶ When you remove the plastic wrap, what do you see in the yogurt carton?

▶ What do you think has been happening inside the bowl?

(To learn more about this investigation and find the answers to the questions, see pages 20–21.)

How much water is in snow?

Sometimes, high in the sky, the air gets so cold that water vapor freezes and turns into tiny **crystals** of ice. The crystals join together to make snowflakes. Then snow, instead of rain, falls from a cloud. If you live in an area that sometimes gets snow, you can investigate how much water snow contains.

You will need:

- A clear glass jar
- Snow
- A ruler
- A notebook and a pencil

1 On a day when there's snow on the ground, go outside and fill a jar with snow.

2 Use a ruler to measure how many inches of snow are in the jar. Record the measurement in your notebook.

▶ When the snow melts, how many inches of water do you predict will be in the jar? Will the level, or depth, of the water be higher, lower, or the same as the level of the snow? Why?

Write your predictions in your notebook.

3 Place the jar of snow indoors in a warm place.

4 Once all the snow melts, measure how many inches of water are in the jar.

In your notebook, write down everything you observed.

▶ How did the amount of the snow compare to the amount of the water?

▶ Did your prediction match what happened?

▶ How can you explain the results?

(To learn more about this investigation and find the answers to the questions, see pages 20–21.)

How can you melt ice when it's cold outside?

When snow falls or ice forms on the ground, roads and sidewalks can become slippery and dangerous. If the temperature rises, the snow and ice will melt. However, what if the weather stays cold? Are there other ways to melt snow and ice? Let's investigate!

You will need:

- A spoonful of salt
- A spoonful of sand
- A spoonful of sugar
- 12 ice cubes that are exactly the same size
- 4 small bowls
- A refrigerator
- A clock
- A notebook and a pencil

1 Look at the salt, sand, and sugar.

▶ Do you think any of these materials could be used to melt ice?

Write your prediction in a notebook.

sand

salt

sugar

2 Put three ice cubes in each bowl.

3 Quickly sprinkle the salt over one bowl of ice cubes. Sprinkle the sand over the second bowl and the sugar over the third. The fourth bowl should just contain ice cubes.

4 Place the four bowls in a refrigerator. Check the bowls every 20 minutes until the ice cubes in all four bowls are completely melted.

▶ Which ice cubes melted first?

▶ Did your prediction match what happened?

(To learn more about this investigation and find the answers to the questions, see pages 20–21.)

How strong is the wind?

Wind is the movement of air. We can't see it, but we can feel its power. Wind can be a gentle breeze that rustles the leaves. It can also be a strong gust that snaps tree branches. In this investigation, you'll build a wind gauge to help you measure the strength of the wind.

You will need:

- Scissors
- A ruler
- Crepe paper
- Construction paper
- Thin fabric (for example, from an old cotton T-shirt)
- Heavy fabric (for example, from an old wool sock)
- Tape
- A wire coat hanger
- A notebook and a pencil

1 Cut a strip of crepe paper, construction paper, thin fabric, and heavy fabric. Each strip should be 2 inches (5 cm) wide and 12 inches (30.5 cm) long. Securely tape the four strips to the bottom of a coat hanger.

2 Go outside and hang the wind gauge from a thin, low-hanging tree branch. Bend the top curved part of the hanger tightly around the branch.

3 For one week, check the gauge in the morning and then again in the afternoon. Observe which strips of material are moving.

Record your observations in your notebook.

▶ Which materials moved when there was a light breeze?

▶ Did the heavy fabric ever move? How would you describe the wind when this happened?

▶ How can knowing the strength of the wind help people plan their day?

(To learn more about this investigation and find the answers to the questions, see pages 20–21.)

How does a tornado form?

Rain, wind, and snow are all common types of weather. A tornado, however, is an extreme and very dangerous kind of weather. Tornadoes form inside thunderstorm clouds and can destroy almost everything in their paths. In this experiment, you'll make a mini tornado in a jar to investigate how this type of weather forms.

You will need:

- A clean, clear plastic jar with a screw-top lid
- Water
- Dishwashing liquid
- Food coloring
- A notebook and a pencil

tornado

a tree damaged by a tornado

1 Fill the jar about three-quarters full with water. Add three drops of dishwashing liquid and three drops of food coloring to the water.

2 Screw the lid onto the jar tightly. Very quickly, swirl the jar around about 20 times in small circular motions. Once you stop swirling, immediately watch what's happening in the jar.

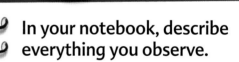

In your notebook, describe everything you observe.

▶ What do you see in the jar? Draw a picture in your notebook.

▶ How do you think what happened in the jar is similar to a real tornado?

(To learn more about this investigation and find the answers to the questions, see pages 20–21.)

Discovery Time

Using science to investigate weather is fun! Now, let's check out all the things we've discovered.

How can the sun help you tell time?

Pages 6-7

When the sun's light is blocked by something, a shadow forms. The pencil on your sundial is blocking light and creating a shadow on the plate. Throughout the day, the sun's position in the sky changes. This makes the shadows change, too. The changing position of the shadow on a sundial during daylight can be used to track the passing hours. At night or on a cloudy day with no sunshine, it's not possible to use a sundial.

How can you measure rainfall?

Pages 8-9

The measurement of the rain will vary, but it will probably be close to what the meteorologist predicted. If 1 inch (2.5 cm) of rain collects in the container, it shows that 1 inch (2.5 cm) of rain has fallen over that area. Without a gauge, it would not be possible to measure the amount of rain that falls because water soaks into the ground.

How does water get into the clouds?

Pages 10-11

There are water drops on the inside of the plastic wrap, and there's water in the yogurt carton. Why? The sun warmed the water in the bowl, and some of the water evaporated, or turned into an invisible gas called water vapor. The vapor floated up and touched the plastic wrap. Then the vapor cooled and turned back into drops of liquid water. Some of the drops fell into the large bowl or the yogurt carton. How is this similar to how rain is made? The sun warms water in puddles, rivers, lakes, and oceans. Some of the water becomes water vapor that floats into the air. High above Earth, the water vapor cools down and turns back into droplets of water, forming clouds. Eventually, the water droplets fall back down to Earth as rain.

How much water is in snow?

The level of the water in the jar was lower than the level of the snow. This is because there are spaces filled with air between the tiny ice crystals that form a snowflake. Also, as snowflakes settle on the ground, more air gets trapped in between them. So the snow in the jar contained lots of air. Once the snow melted, the air escaped from the jar, leaving just a small amount of water.

How can you melt ice when it's cold outside?

The ice cubes sprinkled with salt melted first. Normally, the temperature at which water freezes, or its freezing point, is 32°F (0°C). If salt mixes with water, however, the salt changes the water's freezing point to a lower temperature, making it harder for the water to freeze. If water is already frozen as ice, salt can melt the ice. Sand and sugar do not affect the freezing point of water.

How strong is the wind?

You can measure how strong the wind is by observing which of the materials on your gauge moved. The stronger the wind, the more materials that moved. Knowing the strength of the wind is helpful in many ways. For example, it's easier to fly a kite or ride on a sailboat on a windy day. When there's a very strong wind, a person may decide to wear warm clothes.

- Crepe paper = light breeze
- Construction paper = strong breeze
- Thin fabric = windy
- Heavy fabric = very windy

How does a tornado form?

A tornado forms when winds in a thunderstorm cloud begin to spin. The spinning air moves faster and faster, forming a swirling column called a vortex. By swirling the jar of water again and again in the same direction, you made the water spin faster and faster. Just like air, the water formed a vortex, and for just a few seconds, you could see a mini tornado in your jar.

Weather in Your World

Weather doesn't do exciting things only during scientific experiments. Check out the ways you can see weather in action every day!

1. Meteorologists often forecast the weather for the coming week.

▶ **In what ways are weather forecasts helpful to people?**

Make a list in your notebook. There are some examples to get you started in the answers section at the bottom of this page.

2. After a rain shower, there are often puddles on the ground. When the sun shines, the puddles dry up and disappear.

▶ **Where do you think the water has gone?**

3. During winter in some parts of the country, trucks remove snow from the roads. Some of these trucks also help melt ice on the streets.

▶ **What do you think the trucks spread on the roads to melt the ice?**

4. Sometimes there's thick, white fog floating in the air. This type of weather can make it difficult to see very far.

▶ **What do you think fog is made of?**

Science Words

clouds (KLOUDZ)
masses of tiny water droplets or bits of ice floating in the sky

crystals (KRISS-tuhlz)
solid substances that form into shapes with straight edges and smooth sides

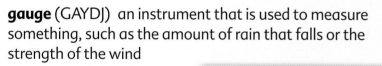

forecast (FORE-kast) to say something will happen in the future, often having to do with the weather

gauge (GAYDJ) an instrument that is used to measure something, such as the amount of rain that falls or the strength of the wind

meteorologists (mee-tee-ur-OL-uh-jists) scientists who study weather and predict, or forecast, what the weather will be today and in the future

predicted (pree-DIKT-ihd)
made a guess, based on facts or observations, that something will happen in a certain way

temperature (TEMP-ur-uh-chur)
a measurement of how hot or cold something is

thermometer (thur-MOM-uh-tur)
an instrument that shows the temperature of something, such as the air

water cycle (WAH-tur SYE-kuhl)
the movement of water from Earth up into the sky to form clouds, and then back down to Earth again as rain or snow

weather (WETH-ur) how hot or cold it is outside, and other conditions such as rain, wind, and snow

Index

Read More

Lawrence, Ellen. *What Is the Water Cycle? (Weather Wise).* New York: Bearport (2012).

Nunn, Daniel. *Weather (True or False?).* Mankato, MN: Heinemann-Raintree (2013).

Owen, Ruth. *Science and Craft Projects with Weather (Get Crafty Outdoors).* New York: Rosen (2013).

Learn More Online

To learn more about weather, visit
www.bearportpublishing.com/FundamentalExperiments

About the Author

Ellen Lawrence lives in the United Kingdom. Her favorite books to write are those about nature and animals. In fact, the first book Ellen bought for herself, when she was six years old, was the story of a gorilla named Patty Cake that was born in New York's Central Park Zoo.